The Battle of Hexham by George Colman the Younger

or, DAYS OF OLD

A PLAY, IN THREE ACTS. AS PERFORMED AT THE THEATRE ROYAL, HAYMARKET.

George Colman the Younger was born on 21st October 1762, the son of George Colman the Elder, a noted and successful playwright and translator of Terence and Plautus among others.

Colman was educated at Westminster School before going on to University at Christ Church, Oxford, and then King's College, University of Aberdeen, before finally proceeding to Lincoln's Inn, London to become a student in Law.

In 1782 his first play 'The Female Dramatist' was premiered at his father's Haymarket theatre.

It appears that as early as 1784, Colman had entered into a runaway marriage with an actress, Clara Morris, to whose brother David Morris, he eventually sold his inherited share in the Haymarket theatre.

After her death he wrote many of the leading parts in his plays for Mrs Gibbs (née Logan), whom he was said to have secretly married after the death of his first wife.

His father, George Colman the Elder, was by now in failing health and was obliged to relinquish to his son the management of the Haymarket theatre in 1789, at a yearly salary of £600. Although Colman sought to emulate and build on the success of his father he was not quite of the same caliber.

On the death of his father in 1794, the Haymarket patent was continued to the son; but difficulties arose in his path, he was involved in litigation with Thomas Harris, and was unable to pay the running expenses of the performances at the Haymarket. In dire circumstances Colman was forced to seek sanctuary within the Rules of the King's Bench Prison. Although he would continue to manage the affairs of the theatre he would reside here for several years.

Released at last through the kindness of George IV, who had appointed him exon. of the Yeomen of the Guard, a dignity that Colman soon liquidated to the highest bidder.

In 1824 he was made examiner of plays by the Duke of Montrose, then the Lord Chamberlain. This granting of office caused widespread controversy amongst his peers who were appalled at his severe censorship and illiberal views, especially as his own works were often condemned as indecent. Apparently at times even the words 'heaven' and 'angel' were deemed to be offensive by him.

George Colman the Younger held this office until his death in Brompton, London on 17th October 1836 at the age of 73. He was buried alongside his father in Kensington Church.

Index of Contents
REMARKS by Mrs Inchbald
DRAMATIS PERSONÆ
SCENE: Northumberland

THE BATTLE OF HEXHAM
ACT THE FIRST
SCENE I. An open Country, near Hexham, in Northumberland; A distant View of Henry the Sixth's Camp.
SCENE II. Henry the Sixth's Camp, at Hexham
SCENE III. Outside of the Royal Tent
SCENE IV. The Field
SCENE V. Open Country
ACT THE SECOND
SCENE I. A Cave, in Hexham Forest
SCENE II. Part of the Forest
SCENE III. Another Part of the Forest
ACT THE THIRD
SCENE I. A Village, on the Skirts of the Forest
SCENE II. An old fashioned Apartment, in Barton's House, in the Village
SCENE III. Another Apartment, in Barton's House
SCENE IV. The Village
GEORGE COLMAN THE YOUNGER – A CONCISE BIBLIOGRAPHY

REMARKS by Mrs Inchbald

Mr. Colman acquaints his readers, in his Preface to this play, dated 1808, that it was written near twenty years ago: then, stating, as an apology to his jocose accusers, this reason for having made Shakespeare the model for his dialogue—that plays, which exhibit incidents of former ages, should have the language of the characters conform to their dress—he adds—"To copy Shakspeare, in the general tournure of his phraseology, is a mechanical task, which may be accomplished with a common share of industry and observation:—and this I have attempted (for the reason assigned); endeavouring, at the same time, to avoid a servile quaintness, which would disgust. To aspire to a resemblance of his boundless powers, would have been the labour of a coxcomb;—and had I been vain enough to have essayed it, I should have placed myself in a situation similar to that of the strolling actor, who advertised his performance of a part"—"In imitation of the inimitable Garrick."

"The Battle of Hexham" has been one of the author's most popular works; and has, perhaps, to charge its present loss of influence with the public, to those historical events of modern times, which have steeled the heart against all minor scenes of woe, and deprived of their wonted interest the sorrows of Queen Margaret and her child.

There is a short, but well known narrative, written by one Clery, an humble valet de chambre—which, for pathetic claims, in behalf of suffering majesty and infant royalty, may bid defiance to all that history has before recorded, or poets feigned, to melt the soul to sympathy.

Nor can anxiety be now awakened in consequence of a past battle at Hexham, between a few thousand men, merely disputing which of two cousins should be their king, when, at this present period, hundreds of thousands yearly combat and die, in a cause of far less doubtful importance.

The loyal speeches of Gondibert, in this play, his zeal in the cause of his sovereign, every reader will admire—yet one difficulty occurs to abate this admiration—Did Gondibert know who his sovereign was?

This question seems to be involved in that same degree of darkness, in which half the destructive battles which ever took place have been fought.

The adverse parties at Hexham had each a sovereign. Edward the Fourth was the lawful king of the York adherents, as Henry the Sixth was of those of Lancaster; and Edward had at least birthright on his side, being the lineal descendant of the elder brother of Henry the Fourth, and, as such, next heir to Richard the Second, setting aside the usurper.—But, possibly, the degraded state of Henry the Sixth was the strongest tie, which bound this valiant soldier to his supposed allegiance;—for there are politicians so compassionate towards the afflicted, or so envious of the prosperous, they will not cordially acknowledge a monarch until he is dethroned.—Even the people of England never would allow the Bourbon family to be the lawful kings of France, till within these last fifteen years 1.

The youthful reader will delight in the conjugal ardour of Adeline; whilst the prudent matron will conceive—that, had she loved her blooming offspring, as she professes, it had been better to have remained at home for their protection, than to have wandered in camps and forests, dressed in vile disguise, solely for the joy of seeing their father.—But prudence is a virtue, which would destroy the best heroine that ever was invented. A mediocrity of discretion even, dispersed among certain characters of a drama, might cast a gloom over the whole fable, divest every incident of its power to surprise, take all point from the catastrophe, and, finally, draw upon the entire composition, the just sentence of condemnation.

It was since the French Revolution that the crown of England relinquished its title and claim to the kingdom of France.

DRAMATIS PERSONÆ

Marquis of Montague	Mr. Gardner.
Duke of Somerset	Mr. Johnson.
A Nobleman	Mr. Iliffe.
La Varenne	Mr. Williamson.
Prince of Wales	Miss Gaudry.
Gondibert	Mr. Bannister, jun.
Barton	Mr. Aickin.
Gregory Gubbins	Mr. Edwin.
Fool	Mr. R. Palmer.
Corporal	Mr. Baddeley.
Drummer	Mr. Moss.
Fifer	Mr. Barret.
First Robber	Mr. Bannister, sen.
Second Ditto	Mr. Davies.
Third Ditto	Mr. Chapman.
Fourth Ditto	Mr. Rees.
Other Robbers	Mr. Mathews, Mr. Chambers, &c.
First Male Villager	Mr. Burton.
Second Ditto	Mr. Painter.
First Female Singing Villager	Mrs. Bannister.
Second Ditto	Mrs. Iliffe.

Margaret	Mrs. S. Kemble.
Adeline	Mrs. Goodall.

Various Robbers, Soldiers, Villagers, &c. &c.

SCENE: Northumberland.

THE BATTLE OF HEXHAM

ACT THE FIRST

SCENE I

An open Country, near Hexham, in Northumberland; A distant View of Henry the Sixth's Camp.

Time: Day-break.

Enter **ADELINE**, in Man's Habit and Accoutrements.

ADELINE
Heigho! Six dark and weary miles, and not yet at the camp. How tediously affliction paces!—Come, Gregory! come on. Why, how you lag behind!—Poor simple soul! what cares has he to weigh him down? Oh, yes,—he has served me from my cradle; and his plain honest heart feels for his mistress's fallen fortunes, and is heavy.—Come, my good fellow, come!

[Enter **GREGORY**.

GREGORY
Mercy on us, how my poor legs do ache!

ADELINE
What, with only six miles this morning?—Fie!

GREGORY
Six!—sixteen, if we've gone an inch; my feet are cut to pieces. A man may as well do penance, with pease in his shoes, as trudge over these confounded roads in Northumberland. I used to wonder, when we were at home, in the south, where it is as smooth as a bowling-green, what the labourers did with all the loose stones they carried off the highways; but now, I find, they come and shoot their rubbish in the northern counties. I wish we had never come into them, with all my heart!

ADELINE
Then, you are weary of my service—you wish you had not followed me.

GREGORY

Who I? Heaven forbid!—I'd follow you to the end of the world:—nay, for that matter, I believe I shall follow you there; for I have tramped after you a deuced long way, without knowing where we are going. But I'd live, ay, and die for you too.

ADELINE
Well, well; we must to the wars, my good fellow.

GREGORY
The wars! O lud! that's taking me at my word with a vengeance! I never could abide fighting—there's something so plaguy quarrelsome in it.

ADELINE
Then you had best return. We now, Gregory, are approaching King Henry's camp.

GREGORY
Are we? Oh dear, oh dear! Pray, then, let us wheel about as fast as we can.

ADELINE
Don't you observe the light breaking through the tents yonder?

GREGORY
Mercy on me! they are tents, sure enough! Come, madam, let's be going, if you please.

ADELINE
Why, whither should I go, poor simpleton? My home is wretchedness. The wars I seek have made it so; they have robbed me of my husband; comfort now is lost to me. Oh! Gondibert, too faithful to a weak cause, our ruin is involved with our betters!

GREGORY
Oh, rot the cause, say I! Plague on the House of Lancaster! it has been many a noble gentleman's undoing. The white and red roses have caused more eyes to water in England, than if we had planted the whole island with onions. Such a coil kept up with their two houses!—one's so old and t'other's so old!—they ought both to be pulled down, for a couple of nuisances to the nation.

ADELINE
Peace! peace, man!—half such a word, spoken at random, might cost your life. The times, Gregory, are dangerous.

GREGORY
Very true, indeed, madam. Death has no modesty in him now-a-days; he stares every body full in the face. I wish we had kept quiet at home, out of his way. Who knows but my master, Lord Gondibert, might have returned to us, unexpectedly; I'm sure he left us unexpectedly enough; for the deuce a bit of any notice did he give us of his going.

ADELINE
Ay, Gregory; was it not unkind? And yet I will not call him so—the times are cruel—not my husband.— His affection had too much thought in it to change. His regular love, corrected by the steady vigour of his mind, knew not the turbulence of boyish raptures; but, like a sober river in its banks, flowed with a

sweet and equal current. Oh! it was such a placid stream of tenderness!—How long is it since your master left us, Gregory?

GREGORY
Six months come to-morrow, madam. I caught a violent cold the very same day: it has settled in my eyes, I believe, for they have been troublesome to me ever since. Ah! I shall never forget that morning; when the spies of the House of York, that's got upon the throne, surrounded him for being an old friend to the Lancasters. Egad, he laid about him like a lion!—Out whips his broad-sword; whack he comes me one over the sconce; pat he goes me another on the cheek; and, after putting them all out of breath, about he wheels his horse, and we have never seen nor heard of him since.

ADELINE
And, from that day to this, I have in vain cherished hopes of his return.—Fearful, no doubt, of being surprised, he keeps concealed.—Thus is he torn from me—torn from his children—poor tender blossoms! too weak to be exposed to the rude tempest of the times, and leaves their innocence unsheltered!

GREGORY
Yes, and mine among the rest. But what is it you mean to do, madam?

ADELINE
To seek him in the camp. The Lancasters again are making head, here, in the north. If he have had an opportunity of joining them, 'tis more than probable he is in their army. Thither will we;—and for this purpose have I doff'd my woman's habit; leaving my house to the care of a trusty friend: and, thus accoutred, have led you, Gregory, the faithful follower of my sorrows, a weary journey half over England.

GREGORY
Weary! oh dear, no—not at all—I could turn about again directly, and walk back, brisker by half than I came.

ADELINE
What, man, afraid! Come, come; we run but little risk. Example, too, will animate us. The very air of the camp, Gregory, will brace your courage to the true pitch.

GREGORY
That may be, madam; and yet, for a bracing air, people are apt to die in it, sooner than in any other place.

ADELINE
Pshaw! pr'ythee, man, put but a confident look on the matter, and we shall do, I warrant. A bluff and blustering outside often conceals a chicken heart. Mine aches, I am sure! but I will hide my grief under the veil of airy carelessness.—Down, sorrow! I'll be all bustle, like the occasion. Come, Gregory! Mark your mistress, man, and learn: see how she'll play the pert young soldier.

SONG.—ADELINE.
The mincing step, the woman's air,
The tender sigh, the soften'd note,

Poor Adeline must now forswear,
Nor think upon the petticoat.
Since love has led me to the field,
The soldier's phrase I'll learn by rote;
I'll talk of drums, of sword and shield,
And quite forget my petticoat.
When the loud cannon's roar I hear,
And trumpets bray with brazen throat,
With blust'ring, then, I'll hide my fear,
Lest I betray my petticoat.
But ah! how slight the terrors past,
If he on whom I fondly dote,
Is to my arms restored at last;—
Then—give me back my petticoat!

[Exit ADELINE.

GREGORY
Well, if I must go, I must. I cannot help following my poor Lady Adeline—affection has led many a bolder man by the nose than I. I wonder, though, how your bold fellows find themselves just before they're going to fight. I wonder if they have any uncomfortable sort of sticking in the throat, and a queer kind of a cold tickling feel in some part of the flesh. Ah! Gregory, Gregory Gubbins! your peaceable qualities will never do for a camp. I never could bear gunpowder, since I got fuddled at the fair, and the boys tied crackers, under Dobbin's tail, in the Market Place.

SONG.—GREGORY GUBBINS.
What's a valiant Hero?
Beat the drum,
And he'll come:—
Row de dow dero!
Nothing does he fear, O!
Risks his life,
While the fife—
Twittle, twittle twero—
Row de dow de dow,
Twittle, twittle twero.
Havock splits his ear, O!
Groans abound,
Trumpets sound,
Ran tan tan ta tero—
Twittle, twittle twero.
Then the scars he'll bear, O!
Muskets roar,
Small shot pour—
Rat tat tat to tero—
Pop, pop, pop,
Twittle, twittle twero.
What brings up the rear, O?

In comes Death;
Stops his breath;—
Good bye, valiant Hero!—
Twittle twittle, rat a tat,
Pop, pop, pop, row de dow, &c. &c.

[Exit.

SCENE II

Henry the Sixth's Camp, at Hexham

Enter a **DRUMMER** and a **FIFER**.

DRUMMER
Morrow to you, Master Tooting—a merry day-breaking to your worship.

FIFER
A sad head-breaking, I fancy. Plaguy troublesome times, brother! Buffetted, by the opposite party, out of one place, and now waiting till they come to buffet us out of another. Whenever they do come, let me tell you, a man will scarce have time to get up from his straw bed, before he's laid down again by a long shot of the enemy. We shall be popp'd at like a parcel of partridges, rising from stubble.

DRUMMER
Pshaw! plague, what signifies taking matters to heart? Luck's all. War's a chance, you know. If one day's bad, another's better. What matters an odd drubbing, or so? A soldier should never grumble.

FIFER
Why, zouns! flesh and blood, nor any thing that belongs to a camp, can't help it. Do, now, only give your drum a good beating, and mind what a damn'd noise it will make.—Not grumble, when we take so many hard knocks?

DRUMMER
No, to be sure; else how should we be able to return them?

FIFER
Ay, there stands the case; we never can return them. Others can have a blow, and give a blow; but as for me, and yourself, and Kit Crackcheeks, the trumpeter; 'sbud, they may thump us from morning to night, and all the revenge we have, is—Toot-a-too, rub-a-dub, and tantararara.

DRUMMER
O fie! learn to know our consequence better, brother, I beseech you. My word for it, we are the heros that do all the execution. Who but we keep up the vigour of an engagement, and the courage of the soldiers? Fear, brother, is, for all the world, like your bite of a tarantula; there's no conquering its effects without music. We are of as much consequence to an army, as wind to a windmill: the wings can't be put in motion without us.

FIFER
Marry, that's true: and if two armies ever meet without coming to blows, nothing but our absence can be the occasion of it. The only way to restore harmony is, to take away our music.

[Enter a **CORPORAL** and **SOLDIERS**.

SOLDIER
Come along, my boys; now for the news!

CORPORAL
Silence!

SOLDIERS
Ay, ay—Silence.

CORPORAL
Hold your peace, there, and listen to what I'm going to inform you—Hem!—Who am I?

ALL SOLDIERS
Our corporal! Alick Puff;—our corporal.

CORPORAL
O ho! am I so?—then obey orders, you riotous rascals, and keep your tongues between the few teeth the civil war has been civil enough to leave you. What! is it for a parcel of pitiful privates to gabble before their superior officer! know yourselves for a set of ignorant boobies, as you are—and do not forget that I am at the head of you.

DRUMMER
But, pr'ythee, good Master Corporal, what news?

CORPORAL
Ay, there it is; good Master Corporal, and sweet Master Corporal, the news? who is to tell you, but I? and what do I ever get by it?

FIFER
Come, come, you shall have our thanks with all our hearts;—we promise you that.

SOLDIER
Ay, ay, that you shall—now for it!

CORPORAL
Then!—You remember your promise?

ALL SOLDIERS
Yes, yes, we do.

CORPORAL

Why, then, you'll all have your throats cut before to-morrow morning.

ALL
How!

DRUMMER
Pshaw! it can't be!

CORPORAL
See there, now! just as I expected.—After all I have imparted, merely for your pleasure and satisfaction, not a man among you has the gratitude to say, thank you, Corporal, for your kind information.

DRUMMER
But, is the enemy at hand?

CORPORAL
No matter, Mum! only when the business is over with you, and you are all stiff in the field, do me the credit to say, afterwards, I was the first that told you it would happen. I, Alexander Puff, corporal to King Henry the Sixth, (Heaven bless him!) in his majesty's camp, at Hexham, in Northumberland.

FIFER
Well, though they do muster strong, we may make Edward's party skip for all that; if we have but justice on our side.

CORPORAL
Well said, Master Wiseacre!—Justice! No, no! Might overcomes right, now a days. Bully Rebellion has almost frightened Justice out of her wits; and, when she ventures to weigh causes, her hand trembles so confoundedly, that half the merits tumble out of the scale.

FIFER
But, still, I say—

CORPORAL
Say no more—but take care of yourself in the battle—that's all.—'Sblood! if the enemy were to find your little, dry, taper carcase, pink'd full of round holes, they'd mistake you for your own fife. But, remember this, my lads. Edward of York has again shoved King Henry from his possessions, and squatted his own usurping, beggarly gallygaskins, in the clean seat of sovereignty; and here are we brave fellows, at Hexham, come to place him on the stool of repentance. And there's our king at the head of us—and there's his noble consort, the sword and buckler, Queen Margaret—and there's the Lord Seneschal of Normandy—and the Lord Duke of Somerset—and the Lord knows who!—The enemy is at hand, with a thumping power; so up, courage, and to loggerheads we go for it.—Huzza! for the Red Roses, and the House of Lancaster.

ALL
Huzza! huzza! huzza!

SONG.—CORPORAL.
My tight fellow soldiers, prepare for your foes;

Fight away, for the cause of the jolly Red Rose;
Never flinch while you live; should you meet with your death,
There's no fear that you'll run—you'll be quite out of breath.
Then be true to your colours, the Lancasters chose,
And the laurel entwine with the jolly Red Rose.

CHORUS
Then be true, &c.
He who follows for honour the drum and the fife,

May perhaps have the luck to get honour for life;
And he who, for money, makes fighting his trade,
Let him now face the foe, he'll be handsomely paid.
Then be true, &c.

The fight fairly done, my brave boys of the blade,
How we'll talk, o'er our cups, of the havock we've made!
How we'll talk, if we once kill a captain or two,
Of a hundred more fellows, that nobody knew.
Then my tight fellow soldiers prepare for your foes.
And the laurel entwine with the jolly Red Rose.

[Exeunt.

SCENE III

Outside of the Royal Tent

Enter **FOOL**.

FOOL
Queen Margaret has sheltered me from the peltings of fortune, this many a year. Now the pelting has damaged my shelter; but still I stick to it. More simpleton I!—to stand, like a thin-clad booby, in a hard shower, under an unroofed penthouse. Truly, for a fool of my experience, I have but little wisdom: and yet a camp suits well with my humour; take away the fighting—the sleeping in a field—the bad fare—the long marches, and the short pay—and a soldier's is a rare merry life.—Here come two more musterers—troth we have need of them—for, considering the goodness of the cause, they drop in as sparingly as mites into a poor's box.

[Enter **ADELINE** and **GREGORY**.

ADELINE
Tremble not now, Gregory, for your life!

GREGORY

Lord, madam, that is the only thing I do tremble for: if I had as many lives as a cat, I must borrow a tenth, I fancy, to carry me out of this place.

ADELINE
Pooh! pr'ythee—we are here among friends. Did you not mark the courtesy of the centinels; who, upon signifying our intentions, bid us pass on, till we should find a leader, to whom we might tender our services?

GREGORY
Ah! and there he is, I suppose.

[Pointing to the **FOOL**.

Mercy on us! he's a terrible looking fellow—his coat has been so pepper'd with musket shot in the wars, that 'tis patch'd from the very top to the bottom.

ADELINE
Tut, tut, man! your fears have made you blind; this motley gentleman's occupation has nothing terrible in it, I'll answer for it—we will accost him. How now, fellow?

FOOL
How now, fool?

ADELINE
What, sirrah? call you me fool?

FOOL
'Faith may I, sir; when you call me fellow. Hail to you, sir, you are very well met. Nay you need not be ashamed of me for a companion; simple though I seem, we fools come of a great family, with a number of rich relations.

ADELINE
Why do you follow the camp, fool?

FOOL
For the same reason that a blind beggar follows his dog;—though it may lead me where my neck may be broke, I can't get on in the world without it. You, sir, I take it, are come, like me, to shoot your bolt at the enemy?

ADELINE
I come, partly, indeed, among other purposes, to offer my weak aid to the army.

FOOL
Your weakness, sir, acts marvellously wisely: you'll be the clean-shaved Nestor of the regiment.

ADELINE
If I could find your leader, I would vouch, too, for the integrity of this my follower, to be received into the ranks.

GREGORY
Oh no, you need not put yourself to the trouble of vouching for me.

FOOL
Right; for your knave, when great folks have occasion for him, is received with little inquiry into his character. Marry, let an honest man lack their assistance, and starving stares him in the face, for want of a recommendation.

ADELINE
Lead us to your General, and you shall be well remember'd by me.

FOOL
Why, as to a General, I can stand you in little stead; but if such a simple thing as a Queen can content you, I am your only man: for being a proper fellow, and a huge tickler up of a lady's fancy, I may chance to push your fortune as far as another. Truly, you fell into good hands when you stumbled on me.

[Flourish.

Stand back, here comes royalty.

[Enter **QUEEN MARGARET, DUKE OF SOMERSET, LA VARENNE, SENESCHAL OF NORMANDY** of Normandy, with **KNIGHTS** and **SOLDIERS**, from the Tent.

DUKE OF SOMERSET
Here, if it please you, madam, we'll debate.
Our tented councils but disturb the King,
And break his pious meditations.

QUEEN MARGARET
True, Duke of Somerset; for some there are
Who, idly stretch'd upon the bank of life,
Sleep till the stream runs dry.—Is't not vexatious,
That frolic nature, as it were, in mockery,
Should in the rough, and lusty mould of manhood,
Encrust a feeble mind!—Well, upon me
Must rest the load of war.—Assist me, then,
Ye powers of just revenge! fix deep the memory
Of injured majesty! heat my glowing fancy
With all the glittering pride of high dominion;
That, when we meet the traitors who usurp it,
My breast shall swell with manly indignation,
And spur me on to enterprise.

LA VARENNE
Oh! happy
The knight who wields his sword for such a mistress.
I cannot but be proud! When late, in Normandy,

Your grace demanded succour of my countrymen,
And beauty in distress shone like the sun
Piercing a summer's cloud—then—then was I
The honour'd cavalier a royal lady
Chose, from the flower of our nobility,
To right her cause, and punish her oppressors.

QUEEN MARGARET
Thanks, La Varenne; our cause is bound to you;
And my particular bond of obligation
Is stamp'd, my lord, with the warm seal of gratitude.
Yours is a high and gallant spirit, lord!
Impatient of inaction, even in peace
It manifests its owner: for, I found you,
In fertile France, (that nurse of courtesy)
Our sex's foremost champion;—in the tournament
Bearing away the prize, that you might lay it
At some fair lady's feet: thus, in rehearsal,
Training the martial mind to feats of chivalry;
That, when occasion call'd for real service,
It ever was found ready—witness the troops
You lead to action.—Say, lords, think you not
That these, our high-bred Normans, mingled with
Our hardy Scottish friends, like fire in flint,
Will, when the iron hand of battle strikes,
Produce such hot and vivid sparks of valour,
That the pale House of York, aghast with fear,
Shall perish in the flame it rashly kindled?

LA VARENNE
No doubt, no doubt!
'Would that the time were come, when our bright swords
Shall end the contest! Since I pledged myself
To fight this cause, delay's as irksome to me,
As to the mettled boy, contracted to
The nymph he burns for, when cold blooded age
Procrastinates the marriage ceremony.

QUEEN MARGARET
The time's at hand, my lord; the enemy,
Hearing of succours daily flocking to us,
Is marching, as I gather, towards our camp—
Therefore, good Seneschal, look to our troops:
Keep all our men in readiness;—ride thro' the ranks,
And cheer the soldiery.—Come, bustle, bustle.
Oh! we'll not fail, I warrant!—How now, sirrah?
[To the **FOOL**]
How came you here?

FOOL

Willy nilly, madam, as the thief came to the gallows. I am a modest guest here, madam, with a poor stomach for fighting, and need a deal of pressing before I fall to. When Providence made plumbers, it did wisely to leave me out of the number; for, Heaven knows, I take but little delight in lead: but here are two who come to traffic in that commodity.

[Points to **ADELINE** and **GREGORY**.

QUEEN MARGARET
How mean you, sir? What are these men?

FOOL
Swelling spirits, madam, with shrunk fortunes, as I take it;—as painful to the owners, as your gouty leg in a tight boot: but if a man's word be not taken in the world, he's forced to come to blows to keep up a reputation. Poverty without spirit lets in the frost upon him worse than a crazy portal at Christmas; so here are a couple of warped doors in the foul weather of adversity, madam, who want to be listed.

QUEEN MARGARET [To **ADELINE**]
I never saw a youth of better promise:
But say, young man, serve you here willingly
In these our wars?

ADELINE
Yes, madam, if it please you;
And, if my youth should lack ability,
I do beseech you, let my honest will
Atone for its defect:—yet I will say—
And yet I would not boast—that a weak boy
May show you that he is zealous in your service:
For tho' but green in years, alas! misfortune
Has sorely wrung my heart!—and the proud world,
(I blush for't, while I utter it)—must know
What 'tis to suffer, ere its thoughtless breast,
Callous in happiness, can warm with feeling
For others in distress.

QUEEN MARGARET
Poor youth! I pity thee.
And for thy willingness, which I esteem
In friendly working more than if thou brought'st
The strength of Hercules to nerve our battle,
Should the just Heavens smile on our enterprise,
I will not, trust me, youth, forget thee.—

[Enter a **MESSENGER**.

Now the news!

MESSENGER
The enemy approaches. On the brow of the next hill, rising a short mile hence,
Their colours wave.

LA VARENNE
Now then for the issue!

QUEEN MARGARET
Ha!—So near! Who is't that leads their power?

MESSENGER
The Marquis of Montague, so please your Majesty.

[Exit.

QUEEN MARGARET
Then he shall find us ready. Now, my lords!
Remember, half our hopes rest on this onset.—
Some one prepare the King.

[A **KNIGHT** enters the Tent.

If on the border
Of England, here, we cut but boldly through
The troops opposed to intercept our passage,
The afterwork is easy:—
Where's my young son!—then, like a rolling flood,
That once has broke its mound, we'll pour upon
The affrighted country, sweeping all before
Our flood of power, till we penetrate
The very heart on't.—
Go, bring the Prince of Wales!—Now, gallant soldiers,
Fight lustily to-day, and all the rest
Is sport and holiday.

[Enter an **OFFICER** with the young **PRINCE**.

My son!—my boy.
Come to thy mother's bosom! Heaven, who sees
The anxious workings of a parent's heart,
Knows what I feel for thee! Alas! alas!
It grieves me sore to have thee here, my child!
The rough, unkindly blasts of pitiless war
Suit not thy tender years.

PRINCE
Why, mother,

Mustn't I be a soldier? And 'tis time
I should begin my exercise—by and bye
'Twill be too late to learn—and yet I wish
That I were bigger now, for your sake, mother.

QUEEN MARGARET
Why, boy?

PRINCE
Oh! you know well enough, for all your asking.
Do you think, if I were strong enough to fight,
I'd let these raw-boned fellows plague you so?

QUEEN MARGARET
My sweet, brave boy!—Come, lords, and gentlemen;
Let us go cheerily to work! If woman,
In whose weak, yielding breast, nature puts forth
Her softest composition, can shake off
Her idle fears,—what may not you perform?
And you shall see me now, steel'd by th' occasion,
So far unsex myself, that tho' grim death
(Breaking the pale of time) shall stride the field,
With slaught'rous step,—and, prematurely, plunge
His dart in vigorous bosoms, till the earth
Is purple-dyed in gore—still will I stand
Fix'd as the oak, when tempests sweep the forest.
But, still, one woman's fear—one touch of nature,
Tugs at my heartstrings—'tis for thee, my child!
—Oh! may the white-robed angel,
That watches over baby innocence,
Hear a fond mother's prayer, and in the battle
Cast his protecting mantle round thee!—On—
Away.

[Exit.

GREGORY
I shall never know how to set about the business I am put upon. Of all the sports of the field, I never went a man shooting before in my life:—and, yet, when the lady, with the brass bason on her head, begins to talk big, there is a warm glow about one, that—gad! I begin to think 'tis courage;—for I don't know how to describe it; and never felt any thing like it before.

[Alarm.

Zouns! no it e'n't—if it is, my courage is of a plaguy hot nature; for the very sound of a battle has thrown me into a perspiration. Oh! my poor mistress's man! Oh! I wish we were at home, and I was comfortably laid up in our damp garret, with a fine twinging fit of the rheumatism.

[Huzza.

Mercy on us!—here's a whole posse, too, coming the other way. I'm in for it! but, if there is such a thing as the protecting mantle they talk'd of, I hope 'tis a pure large one; and there'll be room enough to lap up me, and my mistress in the tail on't.

[Exit.

SCENE IV

The Field

Enter **LA VARENNE**, followed by the **FOOL**.

LA VARENNE
Death and shame!
Are these the rough, and hardy northern men,
That were to back my Normans? Why, they fly,
Like skimming shadows, o'er a mountain's side,
Chased by the sun.

FOOL
True; the heat of the battle is too strong for their cold constitutions.

LA VARENNE
Here, sirrah, take this token to the King:—
Go with your utmost speed: entreat him, quickly,
To bring his forces in reserve. This effort
Restores, or kills, our hope.—Yet I'll fight all out;
I'll shake these pillars of the White-rose House
Till the whole building totters, tho' its fall
Should crush me in the ruins.

[Exit.

FOOL
Well said, Sampson—that's a bold fellow, and I'm on his side. Red roses for ever!

[Enter a **SOLDIER**, of the White Rose Party.

SOLDIER
Now, fellow, speak! tell me who you fight for.

FOOL
Marry, will I, very willingly. Pray canst tell who has the best of the battle?

SOLDIER
The White Rose, to be sure: we are the strongest.

FOOL
Thank you, friend: pass on—I'm on your side.

[Exit **SOLDIER**.

A low clown, now, might stagger at this shifting; but your true, court-bred fool, always cuts the cloth of his conscience to the fashion of the times.

[Exit.

[Enter **GREGORY** and **ADELINE**, hastily.

GREGORY
Run, run, madam! follow a blockhead's advice, and run, or 'tis all over with us.

ADELINE
Whither shall I fly! Fatigue and despair so wear and press me, I scarcely know what course to take.

GREGORY
Take to your legs, madam! Get on now, or we shall never be able to get off. Come, my dear, good, Lady Adeline! Lord! Lord! only to see now, what little resolution people have, that they can't run away when there's danger.

[Shout.

Plague on your shouting! Since they must make soldiers of us—the light troops against the field, say I!

[Exit, running, followed by **ADELINE**.

[Alarm—Shout—and Retreat sounded.

SCENE V

Open Country

Enter the **MARQUIS OF MONTAGUE**, **EGBERT**, and other **LORDS** of the White Rose Party, **SOLDIERS**, &c.

MARQUIS OF MONTAGUE
Cheerly, my valiant friends! the field is ours.
The scatter'd Roses of the Lancasters,
Now deeper tinted, blush a double red,
In shame of this defeat. Oh! this will much
Rejoice King Edward!—Say, has any friend

Made Henry sure?

EGBERT
He is escaped alone, my lord! and Margaret,
Who, with her little son, went, hand in hand,
Hovering about the field, with anxious hope,
Ev'n to the very last; when she perceived
Her lines broke thro'—her troops almost dispersed,—
She hung upon her boy, in silent anguish,
Till the big tear dropt in his lily neck:
Then, kissing him, as by a sudden impulse,
Which mothers feel, she snatch'd him to her bosom,
And fled with her young treasure in her arms:—
Nature so spoke in't, that our very soldiers
Were soften'd at the scene, and, dull'd with pity,
Grew sluggish in pursuit.

MARQUIS OF MONTAGUE
Well, let them go:—
Their cause is, now, become so weak, and sickly,
That, tho' the head exist, to plot fresh mischief,
They will want limbs to execute,—Their House,
(Once strong and mighty,) like a a palsied Hercules,
Must, now, lament it has outlived its powers.—
Meantime, as we return, in pride of conquest,
Let us impress the minds of Englishmen
With new-won glories of the House of York.
Strike drum!—Sound trumpet!—Let the air be rent,
With high and martial songs of victory.

GRAND CHORUS.
Strike!—the God of Conquest sheds
His choicest laurels on our heads:
Mars, with fury-darting eye,
Smooths his brow, and stalks before us;
Leading our triumphant chorus,
Hand in hand, with victory.
And hark! the thund'ring drum, and fife's shrill tone,
With brazen trumpet's clang, proclaim the day our own.

[Huzzas.

ACT THE SECOND

SCENE I

A Cave, in Hexham Forest

ROBBERS are discovered, drinking

OLD GLEE, AND OLD WORDS
When Arthur first, in court, began
To wear long hanging-sleeves,
He entertain'd three serving-men,
And all of them were thieves.
The first he was an Irishman,
The second was a Scot,
The third he was a Welshman,
And all were knaves, I wot.
The Irishman, he loved Usquebaugh,
The Scot loved ale, called blue-cap;
The Welshman he loved toasted cheese,
And made his mouth like a mouse-trap.
Usquebaugh burnt the Irishman,
The Scot was drown'd in ale;
The Welshman had like t' have been choak'd with a mouse,
But he pull'd her out by the tail.

1ST ROBBER
Sung like true and noble boys of plunder! Isn't this free-booting spirit, now, better than leading a cowardly life of musty regularity? Honesty is a scarce and tender commodity, that perishes almost as soon as it appears:—the rich man is not known to have it, for fortune has never put him to the test; and the poor blockhead, that boasts on't, dies for hunger in proving it.

2ND ROBBER
Right; it is but a fever in the blood, that soon kills the patient if it be not expelled.—I had the fever, once.

4TH ROBBER
And what was your cure for't?

2ND ROBBER
Starving. Ever while you live, starve your fever:—when honesty is your case, only call in poverty as physician, and the disease soon yields to his prescriptions.

1ST ROBBER
Pshaw! plague on your physic? aren't we taking our wine in the full vigour of roguery? This it is—

[Holding the Bottle.

—that gives courage to poor knaves to knock down rich fools, in the forest;—just as it gives rich fools spirits to sally forth, and break poor knaves' heads, in the town. Come, as I'm Lieutenant, and our Captain is prowling, let's to business:—read over the list of our yesterday's booties.

2ND ROBBER
Agreed! but, first, one more round; one health; one general health, and then we'll to't.

1ST ROBBER
Here it is then—here's a short, little, snug, general health, that hits most humours; it suits your soldier, your tithe parson, your lawyer, your politician, just as well as your robber.

ALL
Now for it.

[**ALL** rise.

1ST ROBBER
Plunder!

[Drinks.

ALL
Plunder!

[**ALL** drink.

1ST ROBBER
And now for the list.

2ND ROBBER [Reads]
Hexham Forest, May 14th, 1462. Taken, from a single lady, on a pad nag, eleven pounds, four groats, and a portmanteau.—She seemed marvellously frightened, and whispered thanks, privately, for her delivery.

1ST ROBBER
No uncommon case—she isn't the first single lady who has been delivered, and whispered thanks for it in private.

2ND ROBBER
From a Scotch laird, on his way from London to Inverness—by Philip Thunder in gloves; the whole provision for his journey, viz. one cracked angel, and two sticks of brimstone.

1ST ROBBER
Who has his horse?

2ND ROBBER
No one; the Scotch laird travelled on foot. From a pair of justices of the peace, a foundered mare, a black gelding, two doublets, and a hundred marks in gold—they were tied back to back;—

1ST ROBBER
Good! It is but right, that they who bind over so many, should at last, be bound over themselves; and a wise thief is ever bound in justice to put a foolish justice in binding.

2ND ROBBER

Back to back, and hoodwinked—They were left, lamenting their fate, in the forest.

1ST ROBBER

Lament! O villains!—To be in the commission of the peace, and not know that Justice should always be blind. Marry, a good day! Are there any more?

2ND ROBBER

Only a fat friar, who was half plundered, and saved himself by flight.

1ST ROBBER

The better fortune his. Few fat friars, I fancy, have the luck to be saved. What did he yield?

2ND ROBBER

The rope from his middle, a bottle of sack from his bosom, and a link of hog's puddings, pulled out of his left sleeve.

1ST ROBBER

Gad a mercy, friar! For the sack, and the sausages, they shall be shared, merrily, among us; and for the rope,—hum!—come, we won't think of that, now.

[A Horn wound lowly.

Hark! there's our Captain's horn!—'faith, for one who, I suspect is married, he chuses an odd signal of approach.

2ND ROBBER

Nay, though he may be married, he's no milksop; and, I warrant him, when he's on duty, and robbing among us, he quite forgets his wife, as an honest man should do. He has joined us but a short time, yet, egad, he heads us nobly! He'll pluck you an hundred crowns from a rich fellow's pocket, with one hand, and throw his share of them into a hungry beggar's hat, with the other. But, here he comes.

[Enter **GONDIBERT**.

ALL

Hail, noble Captain!

GONDIBERT

How now, my bold and rugged companions! What has been done in my absence?

1ST ROBBER

Oh, sir, a deal of business—We have been washing down old scores, and getting vigour for new. We have had a cup for every breach of the law we have committed. Marry, sir, ours is a rare cellar, to stand such a soaking.

GONDIBERT

Now then, to a business of greater import. I have been lurking round the camp, here, on the skirts of the forest. The parties have met, and a hot battle ensued. It was a long time fought with such stubborn courage, that, as I stood observing it, the spirit of war, pent up within me, had well nigh burst my breast.—Twenty times, I was at the point of breaking from my shelter, and joining combat. But I am pledged to you, my fellows;—that thought restrained me.

2ND ROBBER
O, noble Captain!—but who has conquered?

GONDIBERT
Ay, there it is:—'sdeath and fury, my blood boiled to see it! The sleek, upstart rascals, cut through the ranks as if—oh! a plague on their well feeding!—We had carried it else, all the world to nothing!

2ND ROBBER
We! why what is it to us who has the day? Do but tell us who.

GONDIBERT
I had forgot. The Lancasters are defeated, their soldiers routed, and many of their leaders dispersed about the country. Some, no doubt, are in the forest. Usurping war never glutted on a richer banquet.

1ST ROBBER
Why, it seems to have been a pretty feast; and, the best on't is, now 'tis over, we shall come in for the picking of the bones.

GONDIBERT
It may be so. You all, I know, will expect a rich booty; and they whom we shall meet will, probably, from the unsettled nature of the times, bear their whole wealth about their persons:—but they are brave, and have been oppressed;—disappointment, therefore, and their situation, may cause them to fight in their defence, like heros.

2ND ROBBER
Nay, an they fight like devils, they'll find we can match them in courage. Put me to any proof you please, and they shall soon find me a man.

GONDIBERT
Then, prove it, friend, by pity for the unfortunate. Believe me, comrades, he has little better to boast than a brute, who cannot temper his courage with feeling. And, now, as our expedition is at hand, let each of you observe my orders. If there be any whose appearance denotes a more than common birth, treat him with due respect, and conduct him to my cave. As to the plunder (which our wild life obliges us to exact from the way-worn passenger) on this occasion, pr'ythee, good comrades, take sparingly, and use your prisoners generously.

4TH ROBBER [Half aside, and muttering]
'Sblood! this captain of ours had better take to the pulpit than the road. If he must preach so plaguily about generosity, he might, at least, pay for it out of his own pocket.

GONDIBERT
Who's he that dares to mutter? Come forth, thou wretch! Thus do I punish mutiny, and presumption.

[*Pulls him down, and holds his Sword over him.*

4TH ROBBER
Oh, mercy! good Captain, mercy!

GONDIBERT
Well, take it, though thou deservest none; and learn from this, thou poor, base reptile! how to show mercy to others whom fortune places in thy power. Now, friends, all to your posts. I shall go forth alone. You have your orders, and I know you will obey them strictly. The night steals on us apace; and the angry clouds, threatning a storm, add to the awful gloom of the forest. Away, boys! and be steady.

1ST ROBBER
As rocks, Captain. Come, bullies! all to your duties. Keep your ears, and lose your tongues. Listen, in silence, for the tread of a passenger; and, when he's near enough, spring upon him, like so many cats at a mouse hole.

CATCH.
"Buz, quoth the blue-fly."
Lurk o'er the green-sword;
Mum let us be:—
Lurk, and mum's the word,
For you and me!
Thro' the brake, thro' the wood, prowl, prowl around!
We watch the footsteps, with ears to the ground.
Ears to the ground.

[*Exeunt* **ROBBERS**.

GONDIBERT
Here is another moment snatch'd—a short one—
To commune with myself:—yet, wherefore, think?
Why court consuming sorrow to my bosom,
Which, like the nurs'ling pelican, drinks the blood
Of its fond cherisher?
Why rather should not turbulence of action
Shake off the tax of tyrannous remembrance?
'Tis not the mere, and actual suffering,
That bends the noble spirit to the earth,
And cracks the proud heart's chord:—The prisoner,
Whose feverish limbs, for many a long, long year,
No summer breeze has fann'd, might still be patient,—
Did not remembrance, yoked with cursed comparison,
Enter his dungeon walls, and conjure up
The shadows of past joys;—then, thought on thought,
Like molten lead, run thro' the wretch's brain,
And burning fancy mads him.—Hence, Remembrance!
How baneful art thou to me, when this course

Must be thy antidote! I'll thro' the forest,
And seek these wanderers.—Fell necessity,
And the rude band that I am link'd withal,
Demand that I should prey on them:—yet, still,
My heart leans to them, tho' their fatal cause
Has shorn me to the quick:—for them I fled
My home, my dear loved——Oh, peace, Gondibert!
Touch not that string!—If I must think, I'll think
That Heaven one day may smile.

[Exit.

SCENE II

Part of the Forest

Enter **ADELINE** and **GREGORY**.

GREGORY
Gently, good madam; gently, for the love of corns! Where is it you mean to go?

ADELINE
Even where chance shall carry us, Gregory.

GREGORY
'Faith, madam, and if chance would carry us, it would be doing us a great favour; for we have walked far enough, in all conscience.

ADELINE
Then, here, my good fellow, we must rest ourselves.

GREGORY
Here! what in the wood? and night coming on!

ADELINE
Good faith even here!—here, for necessity demands it, we must pass the night: and, in the morning, the ring-dove, cooing to its mate, will wake us to our journey homeward. This is a retreat, were but the mind at ease, a king might well repose in.

GREGORY
It must be King Nebuchadnezzar then: if we haven't some of his grass-eating qualities, we shall find ourselves badly off for a supper. 'Tis ten to one, too, but we may wander here for a week, without finding our way out again.

ADELINE

Oh! this world! this world! I am weary on't! 'Would I had been some villager!—'twere well, now, to be a shepherd's boy—he has no cares—but while his sheep browse on the mountain's side, with vacant mind—happy in ignorance—he sinks to sleep, o'ercanopied with heaven, and makes the turf his pillow.

GREGORY
Yes, but he has plaguy damp sheets, for all that. I'd exchange all the turf and sky in the county, for a good warm barn and a blanket; and as for the cooing doves, I would not give a crack'd tester for a forest full of them; unless I could see some of their claws stuck up through the holes of a brown piecrust.

ADELINE
Fie! Gregory; be content, be content. Think that we are happy in this forest, in having thus escaped the enemy's fire, and be grateful in the change.

GREGORY
Why, we are out of the fire, to be sure; but, make the best on't we can, we are still in the frying-pan. And starving is one of those blessings for which people are not very apt to be thankful. But we have escaped killing; so I'll e'en be content, as long as there is comfort in comparison. I stumbled over a fat trumpeter in the field, stript and plunder'd, with his skin full of bullets. Well, I am thankful yet—mine is a marvellous happy lot, to be better than a dead trumpeter!

ADELINE
Truce now, Gregory; and consider how we can best dispose ourselves here, till the morning.

GREGORY
Nay, there's no need of much consideration; there's little distinction of apartments here, madam: we shall both sleep on the ground floor—and our lodgings will be pure and airy, I warrant them.

ADELINE
Peace, fool! nor let thy grosser mind, half fears, half levity, thus trifle with my feelings! I have borne me up against affliction, till my o'ercharged bosom can contain no longer.

GREGORY
O the father! look if my poor dear lady be not a weeping!—why, madam—Lady Adeline—dear madam! I am but a fool as you say; but I'm as honest and as faithful as the greatest knave of them all:—and haven't I sighed, sobbed, fasted, fought, and run away, to show you that I would stand by you to the last? and haven't I——

ADELINE
Pr'ythee, no more, Gregory! bear with, my pettishness—for, now and then, the tongue of disappointment will needs let fall some of the acid drops which misery sprinkles the heart withal.

GREGORY
Now must I play the comforter. Why, lord, madam, I think, when a body comes to be used to it a little, this forest must be a sweet, dingy, retired, gloomy, pleasant sort of a place;—besides, what's one night? sleeping bears it out—and I'll warrant us we'll find such snug delicious beds of dry leaves, that—

[Hard shower.

'Sbud! no!—I lie—it rains like all the dogs and cats in the kingdom—there won't be a dry twig left, large enough to shelter a cock-chafer—we shall both be sopped here, like two toasts in a tankard—

[Thunder.

ADELINE
Why, why should fortune sport with a weak woman thus! why, fickle goddess, wanton as boys in giddy cruelty, torture a silly fly before you kill it?

GREGORY
'Faith, madam, for that matter, I am but a blue-bottle of fortune's myself; and, though sorrow is dry, they say, this is a sort of soaking it does not care to be moistened with. If it would rain good barrels of ale, now, sorrow would not so much mind being out in the storm.

[Thunder again.

No; sorrow would be disappointed there too: this rumbling is enough to flatten the finest beer shower, a man would wish to take a whet in.—Lud! lud! madam! let's get out ou't, if there's a hollow tree to be found.

[Thunder.

ADELINE
The thunder rolls awful on the ear, and strikes the soul with terror. The plunderer, too, perhaps catching the sulphurous flash, explores his wretched prey, and stalks to midnight murder.

GREGORY
Mercy on us, madam, don't talk of that!—now I think on't, if we were to pick and chuse, for a twelvemonth, we couldn't have pitched upon a more convenient place to be knocked down in. Shelter! dear madam! shelter.

ADELINE
Is it thus you stand by me, Gregory? I, at least, hoped you had valour enough to—

[**ROBBERS** appear behind, and slowly advance.

GREGORY
Exactly enough; but not a morsel to spare. So we'll e'en look out for a place of safety. Not that I'm afraid though.—Stand by you?—egad, if half a dozen, now, of stout, raw-boned fellows were to dare to molest you, I would make no more of whipping this—

[Drawing his Sword.

—through their dirty lungs, than I would of—

[**ROBBERS** surround **ADELINE** and **GREGORY**.

1ST ROBBER

Stand!

GREGORY
O mercy! mercy! I'm as dead a man as ever I was in my life.

[Drops his Sword, and falls.

ADELINE
Heavens! when will my miseries end! Speak, friends, what would you have?

1ST ROBBER
What you have.

ADELINE
If it is our lives you seek, they are so care worn, that in resigning them, we part with that which is scarce worth the keeping.

GREGORY
'Tis very true indeed. Pray don't take them, gentlemen;—they'll do you no kind of good.

2ND ROBBER
Peace!

1ST ROBBER
Marry, a well favoured boy. Say, youth, whence came you, and whither bound?

ADELINE
I scarce know whither; but I came far inland; sent by my father to the wars; his sword the sole inheritance his age can leave me. This man, a faithful servant of our cottage, in simple love has followed me.

1ST ROBBER
Well, youth; be of good cheer—He, who has little, has little to lose; and a soldier's pocket is seldom much lighter for emptying. Come; you must both with us—bring them to our captain's cave.

[Exeunt **1ST** and **4TH ROBBER**.

GREGORY
Oh lud; oh lud! Dear, good, sweet faced gentlemen!

2ND ROBBER
Peace, dolt! fear not; our captain's honourable!

GREGORY
Nay, that he must be by his company—but sweet, civil, honest gentlemen!

[The **ROBBERS** press them on.

Oh confound these underground apartments! We shall never get out of them alive. Lord! lord! how hard it is upon a man to be forced to walk to his own burying!

[Exeunt **ADELINE** and **GREGORY**, hurried off by the **ROBBERS**.

SCENE III

Another Part of the Forest

Enter **QUEEN MARGARET**, with the Young **PRINCE EDWARD**.

QUEEN MARGARET
Why, that's well done, my boy!—so—cheerly, cheerly!
See, too, the angry storm's subsiding:—what,
Thou canst not be a-weary, Ned?—I know,
Thou'rt more a man.

PRINCE
Sooth, now, my legs ache sadly!
My heart is light and fresh though; and it mocks
My legs for aching. I would I had your legs,
And you my heart.—Your heart, I fear me, mother,
Is heavier far than mine.

QUEEN MARGARET
Dost think so, Ned?

PRINCE
Ay, and I know so too:—for I am in it.

QUEEN MARGARET
My dear, wronged child!

PRINCE
Pr'ythee now, mother, do not grieve for me;—
I warrant I shall live to be a king, yet.

QUEEN MARGARET
Alas! poor monkey! thou hast little cause
To be in love with greatness: thou hast felt
Its miseries full early.

PRINCE
Then, you know
I've all its good to come.

QUEEN MARGARET
May Heaven grant it!
For thou dost promise nobly, boy. This forest
Will screen us from the hatred of our enemies.
Here, till the rage of war has ceased around us,
I will watch o'er thee, Ned; here guard thy life;—
Thy life! the hope, the care, the joy of mine!
And when thy harrass'd limbs have gain'd their pliancy,
We will resume our task: for I must lead thee
A painful walk, across Northumberland,
As far as Berwick, boy; where we may meet,
Again, our Scottish friends. What sayest thou Ned,
Shouldst joy to see thy father there?

PRINCE
Ay, mother;—
And, though we know he has escaped the traitors,
Were we but sure to find him there, I could
Set out directly.

QUEEN MARGARET
Rest a day or two:
For hadst thou strength, the danger that surrounds us
Prevents our venturing.—Come!—on a little—
We will go look some moss-grown cavern out,
And there thou shalt repose thee, sweet.—

[Enter **GONDIBERT**.

Come, boy! come, take my hand—

[**GONDIBERT** approaches, with his Sword drawn.

GONDIBERT
Advance no further.

QUEEN MARGARET
Ha! Who art thou, that comest, with murderous look,
Here, in the dusky bosom of the wood,
To intercept our passage?

GONDIBERT
One of those
Who, stript of all, by an oppressing world,
Now make reprisals: if my looks be dark,
They best explain my purpose.

PRINCE

Fly! fly! mother!
The villain else, will kill us.

QUEEN MARGARET
Let us pass.
Thou know'st us not; else would there so much terror
Still strike thee of our person, that—no matter.
What cause hast thou to stay me?

GONDIBERT
Biting want;—
An oath sworn to my fellows;—disappointment;—
Despair.—I came not here to parley, lady;—quickly,
Yield what you have, or go where I command.

QUEEN MARGARET
Command! base slave! reduced to this!—Command,
From thee? thou worm!

[Making majestically past him, with the **PRINCE**.

GONDIBERT
Nay, nay; you fly not, lady.

[Holds his Sword, over them.

QUEEN MARGARET
Oh, Heaven! my boy! strike not, on thy allegiance!
Save him, I charge thee, fellow! Save my son;—
The son of thy anointed king.

GONDIBERT
My king!

[Drops his Sword at their Feet.

QUEEN MARGARET
Ay, look, and tremble, slave.

GONDIBERT
I do indeed!—
And tho' my sword has never been unsheathed,
Since fate has link'd me to a lawless band,
But to intimidate, not harm the passenger,
I rather would have plunged its naked point
In mine own bosom, than have raised it thus.—
I do beseech your pardon:—and, if aught,
Wherein I may be capable of service,

Can make atonement, you shall find me ready,
Be it at what blind and perilous risk soever:—
For I have heard the fate of this day's battle;
And should a guide, whose dark, and haggard fortune,
Wraps him in humble seeming, be thought worthy,
In this the time's extremity, to direct
Your wand'ring steps, my zeal will prove itself
Warm, and unshaken, madam.

QUEEN MARGARET
Thou makest amends:—
And the strong tide of evils, rushing in,
With rapid force, upon us, well might urge me,
Like sinking men who grasp at idle straws,
To accept thy service. Yet, thou may'st be false,
And lead my boy to his destruction.—Say,—
What sureties, fellow, have I of thy truth?

GONDIBERT
Think on the awe-inspiring air that marks
A royal brow, and makes the trait'rous soul
Shrink at its own suggestion.—And, when care,
With envious weight, invades the diadem,
To aim an injury then—'twere monstrous baseness!
Oh! long, and ever, ever be there seen
A heaven-gifted charm round Majesty,
To draw confusion on the wretch, who, watching
A transient cloud, that dims its lustre, dares
Think on his sovereign with irreverence!
But, more to bind me, madam, to your confidence,
Know, I have been your soldier; and have fought
In this proud cause—some, haply, may remember me—
When fortune's sunshine smiled upon it.

QUEEN MARGARET
Now—
For greatness ever has its summer friends,
Who, at the fall and winter of its glory,
Fly off like swallows—thou'lt betray me.

GONDIBERT
Never.
Wrong me not in your thoughts, beseech you, madam;
For I will serve you truly;—truly guard
Your royal son.—He is but half a subject,
Who, in the zeal, and duty, for his monarch,
Feels not his breast glow for his prince's welfare.
And, in the moment when the time's rough trial

Calls, loudly, on my sworn allegiance,
And summons it to proof, if I abandon either,
May Heaven, when most I stand in need of mercy,
Abandon me!

PRINCE
Let us go with him, mother.

GONDIBERT
I know each turn and foot-path of the forest:—
Can lead you thro' such blind and secret windings,
That will perplex pursuers, till they wander,
As in a labyrinth.—West of this a little,
There stand some straggling cottages, that form
A silent village; and whose humble tops,
Deep shadow'd by the dark o'erhanging wood,
Escape the notice of the traveller.
Thither, so please you, I'll conduct you, madam.
I have a friend,
Lowly but trusty, who shall tend upon you;
While I will scout the country round, to gain
Intelligence of your divided party.

QUEEN MARGARET [Taking up the Sword which **GONDIBERT** dropped]
Then, take my boy!—for I will trust thee, fellow.
I must perforce;—but mark;—for still I doubt:—
If for a moment—mark me, fellow, well!
Thou givest me cause to think thy damn'd intent
Aims at my dear child's life, that very moment,
Tho' that the next should be my last, I'll plunge
Thy weapon to thy heart.

GONDIBERT
Fear not.

QUEEN MARGARET
Lead on.

[Exeunt:—**GONDIBERT** leading the **PRINCE**, and **QUEEN MARGARET** following with the Sword over Gondibert's Head.

ACT THE THIRD

SCENE I

A Village, on the Skirts of the Forest

Enter **FOOL** and a **VILLAGER**.

VILLAGER
Tell me, good fellow, now, I pr'ythee—

FOOL
But wilt thou lend an ear to my tale?

VILLAGER
That will I; all the ears I am worth.

FOOL
Then need not I tell the story:—for, if thou lend'st all thy ears, then thou'lt have none left to hear it.—Wast ever in a battle, old boy?

VILLAGER
No, truly!

FOOL
Then thou art a dead man.

VILLAGER
What, for not being in a battle!

FOOL
Yea, marry,—by the very first rapier that comes in thy way;—for no man can live by the sword but a soldier;—and of soldiers there are three degrees; and three only.

VILLAGER
As how?

FOOL
As thus:—Your hot fighter—your cool fighter—and your fighter-shy.—The last degree makes a wondrous figure, in many muster-rolls.

VILLAGER
Of which last you make one.

FOOL
In some degree.

VILLAGER
And it was that made you run from the battle.

FOOL

Right; running is your only surety. Bully Achilles, the great warrior of old, thought otherwise; and he was vulnerable only in the heel:—now, my heels always insure me from being wounded.—Dost know why Heaven makes one leg of a man stouter than the other?

VILLAGER
No.

FOOL
That he may be able to put the best leg foremost, when there's occasion.

VILLAGER
And you had occasion enough, last night.

FOOL
Truly, had I; and thus came I to your cottage; where I slept on a bare board all night.

VILLAGER
Ah! Heaven knows my lodging is poor enough! but such as it is, you are welcome.

FOOL
Nay, I quarrel not with the lodging; I only complain of the board—and now wouldst thou know my story.

VILLAGER
I would willingly hear of the battle that was lost.

FOOL
Then pr'ythee, ask of those that found it: but, come, I'll e'en tell thee how it was.—Thou hast a wife?

VILLAGER
Yes, forsooth;—that was my old dame you saw at home.

FOOL
Keep her there; for nature plainly intended her for a homely woman—Didst ever quarrel with her before marriage?

VILLAGER
Never.

FOOL
Afterwards, a little?

VILLAGER
Um!—Why, to say the truth, my poor dame has a fine flourish with a cudgel; but people will needs fall out, now and then, when once they come together.

FOOL
That's the very way we lost the battle:—for had the two parties never met, depend on't, one had never cudgel'd the other.

VILLAGER
Mass! thou art a rare fellow in the field!

FOOL
Very rare;—for I never come there but when I can't help it.

SONG.—FOOL.
To arms, to arms, when Captains cry,
With a heigho! the trumpets blow—
To legs, to legs, brave boys, say I!
Heigho;
I needs must go.
Arrows swift begin to fly,
With a heigho! Twang goes the bow—
And soldiers tumble down and die:—
Heigho!
I'll not do so.
Whizzing by come balls of lead;
With a heigho! thump they go.—
Tall men grow shorter by the head;
Heigho!
I'd rather grow.
In time of trouble I'm away;
With a heigho!—ill winds blow;
But always ready at pay day;
Heigho!
Great folks do so.

[Enter another **VILLAGER**.

1ST VILLAGER
Now, goodman Hobs, whence come you?

2ND VILLAGER [To the **FOOL**]
There is a great lord come in, from the routed party, who has taken shelter in our village, since break of day. One of your great friends, good sir.

FOOL
Didst see him! how look'd he?

2ND VILLAGER
I tended him, some quarter of an hour:—troth, he seem'd wondrous weary.

FOOL
Of thy company.—Now could I be weary too, and find in my heart to be dull:—but here come females; and, were a man's head emptier than a spendthrift's purse, they will ever bring something out on't.

Hence comes it, that your dull husband's head is improved by your lively wife:—if she can bring out nothing else, why she brings out horns.

[Enter **VILLAGERS**, Male and Female.

Now, good folk, whither go you?

3RD VILLAGER
Truly, sir, this is our season for making of hay; and here am I, sir, with the rest of our village, going about it.

FOOL
Now might I, were it not for disgracing the army, turn mower among these clowns;—and why not? Soldiers are but cutters down of flesh, and flesh is grass, all the world over. I'll e'en out, this morning, and do execution in the field.—Come, lads and maidens! One roundelay, and we'll to't!

SONG AND CHORUS OF VILLAGERS.
1ST WOMAN
Drifted snow no more is seen;
Blust'ring Winter passes by;
Merry Spring comes clad in green,
While woodlarks pour their melody.
I hear him! hark!
The merry lark,
Calls us to the new mown hay,
Piping to our roundelay.

2ND VILLAGER
When the golden sun appears,
On the mountain's surly brow;
When his jolly beams he rears,
Darting joy—behold them now!—
Then, then, oh, hark!—
The merry lark
Calls us to the new mown hay,
Piping to our roundelay.

3RD VILLAGER
When the village boy, to field,
Tramps it with the buxom lass,
Fain she would not seem to yield,
Yet gets her tumble on the grass:
Then, then, oh, hark!
The merry lark,
While they tumble in the hay,
Pipes alone his roundelay.

4TH VILLAGER

What are honours? What's a court?
Calm content is worth them all:—
Our honour lies in cudgel sport;
Our brightest court a green-sward ball.
But then—oh hark!
The merry lark,
Calls us to the new mown hay,
Piping to our roundelay.

[Exeunt.

SCENE II

An old fashioned Apartment, in Barton's House, in the Village

Rusty Arms, and other Military Paraphernalia hanging up, in different Parts; &c.

LA VARENNE and **BARTON**.

BARTON
Nay, sir, thank not me:
I am no trader, I, in empty forms;
In neat congees, and kickshaw compliments;
In your,—"Dear sirs," and "Sir, you make me blush;"—
I'm for plain speaking; plain and blunt; besides,
I've been a soldier:—and, I take it, sir,
You, who are still in service, are aware
That blushing seldom troubles the profession.

LA VARENNE
Still, friend, I thank thee.—Thou hast shelter'd me,
At a hard trying moment, when the buffets
Of tainting fortune rather would persuade
Friends to shrink back, than serve me.

BARTON
'Faith, good sir,
I know not how you have been buffetted:—
But this I know,—at least I think I know it—
If there's a soldier, in the world's wide army,
Who will not, in the moment of distress,
Stretch forth his hand to save a falling comrade,
Why, then, I think, that he has little chance
Of being found in Heaven's muster-roll.

LA VARENNE

I like thy plainness well.

BARTON
Nay, sir, my plainness
Is such as Nature gave me: and would men
Leave Nature to herself, good faith, her work
Is pretty equal;—but we will be garnishing;
Until the heart, like to a beauty's face,
Which she ne'er lets alone till she has spoil'd it,
Is so befritter'd round, with worldly nonsense,
That we can scarcely trace sweet Nature's outlines.

LA VARENNE
Who of our party, pr'ythee, since the battle
Have shelter'd here among the villagers?—
Canst tell their names?

BARTON
Ay, marry, can I, sir.
But can and will are birds of diff'rent feather.
Can is a swan, that bottles up its music,
And never lets it out till death is near;
But will's a piping bullfinch, that does ever
Whistle forth every note it has been taught,
To any fool that bids it. Now, sir, mark;—
Whoever's here, would fain be private here;
Whoever's here, depend on't, tell I can;—
Whoever's here, depend on't, tell I will not.

LA VARENNE
Why, this is over-caution!—would not they
Rejoice as readily at seeing me,
As I at seeing them?

BARTON
I know not that:
I am no whisper-monger;—and if, once,
A secret be entrusted to my charge,
I keep it, as an honest agent should,
Lock'd in my heart's old strong box; and I'll answer
No draught from any but my principal.

LA VARENNE
If now thou hast a charge, old trusty, I,
(Believe me), am next heir to't.

BARTON
Very like.

Yet, sir, if heirs had liberty to draw
For what is not their own, till time shall give it them,
I fear the stock would soon be dry;—and, then,
The principals might have some cause to grumble.

LA VARENNE
Thou art the strangest fellow! What's thy name?

BARTON
Barton;—that I may trust you with.

LA VARENNE
No more?

BARTON
No, not a pin's point more. Pshaw! here comes one,
To let all out. Children, and fools, and women,
Will still be babbling.

[Enter **PRINCE EDWARD**.

PRINCE
Oh! my lord, is't you!

LA VARENNE
Oh, my young sir! how my heart springs to meet you!
Where is your royal mother? is she safe?

PRINCE
She's in this house, my lord.—Last night,
This honest man received us:—and another,—
His friend—not quite so honest as he might be—
Did bring us hither;—'twas a rogue, my lord;—
Yet no rogue neither;—and, to say the sooth,
The rogue, my lord, 's a very honest man.
Lord, how this meeting will rejoice my mother!
And she was wishing, now, within this minute,
To see the Seneschal of Normandy.

BARTON
So!
This is the Seneschal of Normandy!
Here is another secret.—Plague take secrets!
This is in token of their liking me;—
Just as an over hospitable host,
Out of pure kindness to his visitor,
Crams the poor bursting soul with meat he loaths.

LA VARENNE
I cannot blame thee, friend;—thou knew'st me not:
And, thou hast, now, a jewel in thy care,
Well worth thy utmost caution in preserving.

BARTON
I need not to be told the value on't.
I have been sworn his mother's subject, sir; and since
My poor house has been honour'd with her presence,
The tender scenes, I've been a witness to,
'Twixt her, and this young bud of royalty,
Would make me traitor to humanity,
Could I betray her. There is a rapturous something,
That plays about an English subject's heart,
When female majesty is seen employ'd
In these sweet duties of domestic love,
Which all can feel,—but very few describe!

LA VARENNE [To **BARTON**]
Oh! how thou warm'st me, fellow, with thy zeal!
Come, my young lord!—now lead us to her majesty.

BARTON
Why, as things are, I'll lead you where she is:—
But were they otherwise, and you had not
Discover'd where she is—you'll pardon me—
But I had led you, sir, a pretty dance
Ere I had led you to her. Come, I'll conduct you.

[Exeunt.

SCENE III

Another Apartment, in Barton's House

Enter **GONDIBERT** and **ROBBER**.

GONDIBERT
Away all night! What then? Am not I their leader? Do they begin to doubt me? Am not I, as it were, wedded to the party?

ROBBER
Very true, noble captain: and we have treated you as a wife would a kind husband:—but when a husband is out all night—why—

GONDIBERT

Well, sir;—what then?

ROBBER
Marry, then, the wife is apt to grumble a little; that's all.

GONDIBERT
Go to;—I had reason. What's the news?

ROBBER
The news is, we have taken some stragglers, in the forest.

GONDIBERT
Are they of note?

ROBBER
'Faith, we have some of all qualities;—gentle and simple mixed:—we had no time to stand upon the picking:—they're all penn'd up in the back cavern;—and you must e'en take 'em like a score of sheep—fat and lean together. But, there is a beardless youth, follow'd by a cowardly serving man, who presses hard to see you.

GONDIBERT
What would he?

ROBBER
'Faith, sir, he would be a noble fellow. I take it he has a great soul, too large for the laws;—he has questioned me plentifully concerning you.

GONDIBERT
Concerning me?

ROBBER
Yes; he inquired if you were married; how long you had been with us; your age; your stature; nay, he was particular enough to ask what sort of a nose stood on your face.

GONDIBERT
Wherefore these questions?

ROBBER
Troth, I think he would like well to serve in our band; for he seems to have a marvellous nice notion of honour. He took up your dagger, of curious workmanship, that lies on your table, in the cave, and did so study the dudgeon on't!—Marry, the boy knows how to handle a weapon, I'll warrant him.

GONDIBERT
Where have you bestowed him?

ROBBER

Why, he was so importunate, that I have brought him, and his man, hither along.—The man, I feared, might babble: so, I've entrusted him to your friend Barton, here; and he, finding he has been a butler, has locked him in the cellarage.

GONDIBERT
Conduct the youth hither.

[Exit **ROBBER**.

Then why should I repine? since there are others,
Who, in the early spring, and May of life,
Behold the promised blossoms of their hope
Nipt in the very bud. Here comes the youth;—
And bears a goodly outside;—yet 'tis a slender bark,
That Providence ne'er framed for tossing much
In a rough sea of troubles.

[Enter **ROBBER** with **ADELINE**.

ROBBER Here, youth; this is our captain. Cheer up now, and speak boldly. You need not fear.—A raw youth, captain, but a mettled one, I'll warrant him.—A word with you.

[Takes **GONDIBERT** apart.

ADELINE
It is, it is my lord!—Oh Heaven! my heart!—to find him thus, too!—Yet, to find him any how is transport.

ROBBER I shall look to it.—You would be private now, I take it.—Now, youth, plead, cleverly, to get admitted among us, and your fortune's made. Be but a short time with us, and it will go hard, indeed, if all your cares, in this world, are not shortly at an end.

[Exit.

GONDIBERT
Now to your business, youth.

ADELINE
'Tis brief.—I have been sorely wrung, sir, by the keen pressure of mishap.—I once had friends: they have left me. One whom I thought a special one—a noble gentleman—who pledged himself, by all the ties that are most binding to a man, to guard my uninstructed youth—even he, to whom my soul looked up; whom, I might say, I loved as with a woman's tenderness,—even he has, now, deserted me.

GONDIBERT
Then he acted basely.

ADELINE
I hope not so, sir.

GONDIBERT
Trust me, I think he did, youth; for there is an open native sincerity that marks thy countenance, which I scarce believe could give just cause to a steady friend to leave thee.

ADELINE
Now, by my holy dame, he had none to suspect me. Yet, from the pressure of the time,—some trying chance—but, I am wandering. This is my suit to you.—If you should find me fit to be entrusted with the secrets of your party, I could wish to be enrolled among you.

GONDIBERT
Hast thou well weigh'd the hardships which our life
Constrains us to? Our perils; nightly watchings
Our fears, disquietudes; our jealousies,
Even of ourselves?—which keep the lawless mind
For ever on the stretch, and turn our sleep,
To frightful slumbers;—where imagination
Discovers, to the dull and feverous sense,
Mis-shapen forms, ghastly and horrible;—
And mixes, in the chaos of the brain,
Terrors, half real, half unnatural;—
Till nature, struggling under the oppression,
Rouses the sleeping wretch,—who starts, and wipes
The chilly drop from off his clay-cold temples;
And fain would call for help, yet dares not utter,
But trembles on his couch, silent and horror struck!

ADELINE
Attempt not to dissuade me; I am fix'd.
Yet there is one soft tie, which, when I think
The cruel edge of keen necessity
Has cut asunder, almost bursts my heart.

GONDIBERT
What is it, youth?

ADELINE
That, which from my youth,—
For I have scarcely yet told one and twenty,—
Might, haply, not be thought;—yet so it is;—
Know, then, that I am married.

GONDIBERT
Married, didst say?
And dost thou love—

ADELINE
Oh! witness for me, Heaven!
The pure and holy warmth that fills my bosom.

GONDIBERT
Nay then, my heart bleeds for thee! for thou mightst
As easily attempt to walk unmov'd,
With all the liquid fires which Ætna vomits
Pour'd in thy breast, as here to hope for happiness.
Oh! what does the heart feel, that's rudely torn
From the dear object of its wedded love!
And, still, to add a spur to gall'd reflection,
That very object, whom the time's necessity
Mads you to part with, witless of the cause,
Arraigns your conduct.

ADELINE [With emotion]
And have you felt this!

GONDIBERT
I tell thee wretched youth—fie! thou unman'st me.—
Pr'ythee, return, young man!—I have a feeling,—
A fellow feeling for thee;—if thou hop'st
For gentle peace to be an inmate with thee,
Turn thy steps homeward;—link not with our band.

ADELINE
Wherefore should I return? return to witness
The bitter load of misery, which circumstance
Has brought upon my house? My infant children—

GONDIBERT
And hast thou children then?
Whose innocence has oft beguil'd thy hours;
Who have look'd smiling up into thy face,
Till the sweet tear of rapturous content
Has trickled down thy cheek?—Thou trying for tune!
Mark out the frozen breast of apathy,
And tho' 'twere triple cased in adamant,
Throw but this poisonous shaft of malice at it,
'Twill pierce it thro' and thro'.

ADELINE
An if I thought 'twere so?—

GONDIBERT
Hear me, young man:—
Thou wring'st a secret from me, which, till now,
Was borne in silence here; while, vulture-like,
It preys upon my vitals.—I am married:—
I have a wife—and one whom kindly nature

Form'd in her lavish mood:—Oh! her gentle love
Beam'd through her eyes, whene'er she turn'd them on me,
With such a mild and virtuous innocence,
That it might charm stern murder!—and yet I
Have wounded, villain like, her peace. Even I,—
In whom her very soul was wrapt—
Turn'd coward with the time, have basely left her.
But I am punish'd for't:—day, night,—asleep,
Awake,—still, or in action,—bleeding fancy
Pictures my wife, sitting in patient anguish;
Pale; mild in sufferance; mingling meek forgiveness
With bitter agony;—blessing him who wrongs her;—
While my poor children, my deserted little ones,
Hang on her knees, and watch the silent drops
Steal down her grief-worn face!—Yea, dost thou weep?
Shape thy course homeward then; for pangs like mine,
Would so convulse thee, youth, that, like an engine,
'Twould wrench thy tender nature from its frame,
And pluck life with it.

ADELINE
Oh! my dear, loved lord!
Here cease those pangs;—here, in the ecstacy of joy,
Behold your Adeline, now rushing to the arms
Of a beloved husband.

[Running into his Arms.

GONDIBERT
Merciful Heaven!
My Adeline! And hast thou!—Oh, my heart!
This sudden conflict!—thus let me clasp thee to it;
Ne'er to part more, till pangs of death shall shake us.
What hast thou suffer'd, sweet!—for me to cause—
And are our children—?

ADELINE
Well, and in safety.

GONDIBERT
And, to leave them too!

ADELINE
Nay, pr'ythee, now, no more of this:—
Blot from thy memory all former sorrow:—
Or, if we think on't, be it at some moment,
When calm content smiles round our happy board.
And, trust me, now, I think our storms are over:—

For, on my way, I learn, the House of York
Has now sent forth free pardon to all those,
Who, long attach'd to the Lancastrian party,
Have not engaged in their late enterprise.

GONDIBERT
Blessed chance,
That now constrain'd me to inaction! Adeline!
Once more to hold thee! to return to happiness—
To see our children!—

[Enter **1ST ROBBER**.

How now! What's the matter?

1ST ROBBER
Marry, the matter is, with the oaf in the cellar; the fool shakes as though he were in an ague; we may e'en turn him adrift any how, for he will no how turn to our profit. He's cowardly and poor; he can neither rob, nor be robbed.

ADELINE
Oh! 'tis my man: I pray you conduct him hither.

1ST ROBBER
I'll trundle him in; but you will make nothing of him. I have been trying to talk him into service, and make him fit for our party; but there are some manner of men 'tis impossible to work any good upon.

[Exit.

ADELINE
Poor simpleton! 'tis Gregory, who, in pure zeal, and honest attachment, has followed me.

[Enter **GREGORY**.

GREGORY
Mercy on us! this is the great cock captain of the whole brood of banditti! 'Tis all over! and I have been shut up, these two hours, like a calf for killing. Lord! lord! if calves did but know the reason for their being stalled, as I have been, they'd so fall away with fear, that veal would not be worth the taking to market.

GONDIBERT
Why, how now, man?

GREGORY
Oh lud! I am a poor fellow, sir; that shall be a longtime getting rich, and would fain not die till I am so. Take my life, sir, and you take all;—I carry it about me, as a snail does his house:—and, truly, sir, you'll find that time has a mortgage upon it of forty-two years, and the furniture, of late, is so worn with ill

usage, that the remainder of the lease is not worth your acceptance:—if, sweet, noble, sir, you would but—

[During this Speech, **GREGORY** has been gradually raising his Eyes from the Ground, till he fixes them on Gondibert's Face.

Eh!—Oh!—O, the father!—No!—Yes—Oh lud—Oh lord!

GONDIBERT
Why, dost not know me, Gregory?

GREGORY
Huzza!—He's found!
[Capering]
Dear my lord, I never was happier since I was born, at the sight of you.

GONDIBERT
Trust me, I think so, Gregory
Come, love;

Let's in for calmer conference. Follow, good Gregory.

[Exeunt **ADELINE** and **GONDIBERT**.

GREGORY
Here's a simple change in a man's fortune! Now might I, when I say 'tis he—were it not as plain 'tis he as a nose is a nose—swear that my eyes were putting a lie in my mouth, in very spite of my teeth.—Oh, the quiet, comfortable days that I shall see again! Mercy on me! 'Tis enough to make a coward tremble, to think on the battles my valour has been put to. Nothing, now again, but old fare, old rubbing of spoons, and a cup of old sherry, behind the old pantry door, to comfort my nose, in a cold frosty morning.

SONG.
"Moderation and Alteration."
In an old quiet parish, on a brown healthy old moor,
Stands my master's old gate, whose old threshold is wore
With many an old friend, who for liquor would roar,
And I uncork'd the old sherry—that I had tasted before.
But it was in Moderation, &c.

There I had an old quiet pantry, of the servants was the head;
And kept the key of the old cellar, and old plate, and chipp'd the brown bread.
If an old barrel was missing, it was easily said,
That the very old beer was one morning found dead:—
But it was in Moderation, &c.

But, we had a good old custom, when the week did begin,
To show, by my accounts, I had not wasted a pin;—
For my lord, tho' he was bountiful, thought waste was a sin;

And never would lay out much, but when my lady lay-in.
But still it was Moderation.

Good lack! good lack! how once Dame Fortune did frown!
I left my old quiet pantry, to trudge from town to town;
Worn quite off my legs, in search of thumps, bobs, and cracks on the crown,
I was fairly knock'd up, and very near foully knock'd down.
But now there's an Alteration,
Oh! it's a wonderful Alteration!

[Exit.

SCENE IV

The Village

Enter **QUEEN MARGARET**, **LA VARENNE**, and **PRINCE**.

QUEEN MARGARET
The northern coast beset!

LA VARENNE
Close watch'd with enemies:—'twere too bold a risk,
That way to seek the sea: then bend your course
Thro' Cumberland, so please you.—
At Solway Frith, we have warm friends, to favour
Your embarkation—Sailing, thence to Galloway,
With all convenient speed, we march towards Edinburgh;
And thitherward, I learn, the king has fled:
Where, in the bosom of the Scottish court,
You may in safety sojourn, till the succour
Which noble Burgundy, warm in beauty's cause,
Once more, no doubt, will lend, again shall plume
The wing of majesty.

QUEEN MARGARET
Then, let sharp injury
Subdue base minds alone; its scalding spirit,
Pour'd in a royal breast, will quicken vengeance.
Why, worthy Seneschal, there's hope in't still!
Holds it not likely,
When our dispersed nobility shall hear,
We are again on foot, our royal standard
Will be so flock'd with friends!—
Here comes the fellow, whom I told you of.

[Enter **GONDIBERT**, **ADELINE**, and **GREGORY**, behind.

Now, good friend, the news?

GONDIBERT
Thus, as my spies inform me, madam:—Montague
Has march'd right north; towards Dunstaburgh; hoping
There to surprise your Majesty—

QUEEN MARGARET
Let the fool on.—
This favours our intended march, through Cumberland.
What else?

GONDIBERT
No more; but that some twenty,
Or thereabout, of your dispersed soldiers
Are fall'n into my power. I have ventured,
Finding, that, here, the village is attach'd,
In honest bonds of loyalty, to direct
My men to march them hither: if your course
Should need a secret guard, these few will serve,
When more were dangerous.

QUEEN MARGARET
Oh, true, true fellow!
Believe me, honest friend, of all the bolts,
Which spiteful fortune hurls against my crown,
None strike so deeply, as my poor ability
Now to requite thy faith.

GONDIBERT
The subject, madam,
Who, in his poor endeavour, can relieve
A sovereign from distress, they, who are loyal,
Will pour down blessings on him; that requital
Threefold o'erpays his services. But here,
Heaven has, in pity of me, now pour'd balm
Upon my bleeding sufferings.

QUEEN MARGARET
What, my young warrior!

ADELINE
A weak one, madam;—and a woman too.
Your pardon, madam, if, to seek a husband,—
Happy has been my search—more than the cause,
Altho' my heart is warm in't—brought me hither.

GONDIBERT
Your guard approaches, madam, and the villagers,

[Enter **KNIGHTS** and **SOLDIERS**.

Anxious, in zeal, to see their royal mistress,
In throngs have follow'd.

[Enter **VILLAGERS**, Male and Female, on each Side.

QUEEN MARGARET
This is a cheering sight!
Soon may this warmth be general; and may Henry
Bask in its genial sunshine.—England, awhile, farewell!
And if in future times—no doubt 'twill be so—
Thy King unite his people to his confidence,
And his commanding virtues, mild, yet kingly,
Shall draw the breath of rapturous loyalty
From the gilt palace to the clay-built cottage,
Then will thy realm, indeed, be enviable.
Strike!—Then on.

[Procession of **SOLDIERS**, and Grand Chorus of **VILLAGERS**.

Sea-girt England, fertile land!
Plenty, from her richest stores,
Ever, with benignant hand,
Her treasure on thy bosom pours.
England! to thyself be true;
When thy realm is truly blest,
'Tis when a monarch's love for you
Is by your loyalty confest.

George Colman the Younger – A Concise Bibliography

The Female Dramatist (1782)
Two to One (1784)
Turk and No Turk (1785)
Inkle and Yarico (1787)
Ways and Means (1788)
The Battle of Hexham (1793)
The Iron Chest (1796)
The Heir at Law (1797)
The Poor Gentleman (1802)
John Bull, or an Englishman's Fireside (1803)

Colman was also the author of a great deal of so-called humorous poetry (usually coarse, though popular) – My Night Gown and Slippers (1797), reprinted under the name of Broad Grins, in 1802; and Poetical Vagaries (1812). Some of his writings were published under the assumed name of Arthur Griffinhood of Turnham Green.

www.ingramcontent.com/pod-product-compliance
Lightning Source LLC
Chambersburg PA
CBHW051704040426
42446CB00009B/1291